# TO BE A PRINCESS

## THE FASCINATING LIVES OF REAL PRINCESSES

*I a princess, king-descended, decked with jewels, gilded drest,*
*Would rather be a peasant with a baby at her breast,*
*For all I shine so like the sun . . .*

FROM "A ROYAL PRINCESS" BY CHRISTINA ROSSETTI

BY HUGH BREWSTER AND LAURIE COULTER
WITH PAINTINGS BY LAURIE McGAW

A HarperCollins*Publishers*/
Madison Press Book

# CONTENTS

# RIVAL SISTERS
## *Mary and Elizabeth Tudor*

PRINCESS MARY WAS furious. The household was moving again. And again, they were planning to humiliate her. In the courtyard of the redbrick palace of Hatfield, porters lugged heavy chests to be loaded onto carts. Several nursemaids fussed with linens and cushions for the velvet litter that would carry Mary's baby half sister, Elizabeth. Uniformed guardsmen stood by, preparing to march at the front of the procession with Elizabeth's litter on their shoulders. And Mary would be expected to walk behind in the mud, like a servant. The countryfolk who had once cheered her as Princess of Wales, King Henry's only daughter, now could not even call out, "Hail, Princess!" without fear of punishment.

This was all the Midnight Crow's doing. Mary couldn't bear to use Anne Boleyn's real name. Nor would she ever call her queen. Mary's mother, Catherine, was England's rightful queen. In the last letter she had been allowed to send to her daughter, Catherine had urged Mary to remain silent and obey the King "until this troublesome time be past."

But this troublesome time was not passing quickly. Seven years ago, at the age of eleven, Mary had become aware of the gossip about her parents. She had overheard courtiers whisper that her father was bewitched by one of her mother's ladies-in-waiting, that the King wanted to set aside her mother and marry the beautiful, black-haired Anne Boleyn.

Mary knew the King couldn't marry Anne Boleyn. Divorce was against the laws of the Church. The Pope would never allow it. But soon Mary began to hear a more frightening word—"annulment." King Henry wanted the Pope to dissolve

*Mary waits in front of Hatfield House (opposite) as a nurse brings Elizabeth outside.*

*(Above) The rose was a symbol of the Tudor monarchy.*

his marriage to Catherine so he could marry a younger wife who might bear him a son and heir.

When Mary was seventeen, the unthinkable happened. After the Pope refused to grant the annulment, a furious Henry forced the English clergy to allow him to end his marriage to Catherine. Mary would never forget the terrible day she was told that King Henry and Anne Boleyn were now man and wife, and that Queen Catherine had been banished to a remote and dismal castle. Worst of all, she was soon told that she could not visit her mother or even send letters to her.

But more terrible days were to come. On September 7, 1533, Mary had been summoned to the palace at Greenwich for the birth of Anne Boleyn's child. When her father heard that the newborn was a girl, and not the boy that the soothsayers had promised him, he flew into a mighty rage. Even so, Mary soon heard the sound of trumpets in the next room. A herald announced that the King's new daughter would be known as Princess of Wales and heir to the throne. The following day she heard that the King planned to name his new daughter Mary. *Her* name! The Midnight Crow's daughter was to have both her title and her name!

But something must have changed the King's

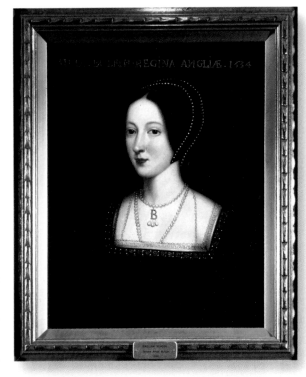

*Anne Boleyn was only twenty-six when she married forty-two-year-old Henry VIII and became queen.*

mind, for at her christening the little red-haired infant was named Elizabeth. Three months later, a splendid royal procession transported the baby Elizabeth to the palace of Hatfield. It was the custom for royal children to be raised away from their parents. Since the age of three, Mary, too, had been the center of a royal household staffed with tutors, ladies-in-waiting and governesses, and more than 160 servants who wore uniforms in blue and green, her own special colors.

A few months after Elizabeth's birth, Mary received a letter from one of the King's officials. It stated that she was to be taken to Hatfield to live as a lady of the household attending the new Princess of Wales. Turning the letter over, she saw that it was addressed to "the Lady Mary, the King's daughter." She was no longer even a princess? This could not be!

The Midnight Crow resented Mary as a possible rival to her own daughter. She was also angry that Mary would not recognize her as queen. Living in the infant Elizabeth's household would teach her a lesson. Two Boleyn relatives, Sir John and Lady Shelton, were in charge of the household at Hatfield. Mary was given the worst rooms in the palace. If Mary refused to call Elizabeth "the Princess of Wales," Lady Shelton was instructed by the Midnight Crow to slap her.

When visitors came to the palace, Mary was to be locked in her room.

After many months of this miserable treatment, Mary was not sorry to be leaving Hatfield with the rest of the household so that the palace could be cleaned. But she dreaded the coming journey. When she saw a groom carrying a saddle across the courtyard, an idea came to her. She would ride to Greenwich! Lady Shelton stared coldly as Mary requested the use of a horse. But she warily nodded her assent. A groom helped Mary into the saddle atop a young mare and she felt her spirits rise. When the procession began to move forward, she dutifully reined her horse in behind the velvet litter bearing Elizabeth. But once they had cleared the palace gates, she suddenly spurred her horse and dashed on ahead. She heard shouts behind her but pressed on.

As Mary galloped down country lanes, people working in the fields looked up, some raising their arms in greeting. Before long, the rooftops of Greenwich came into view. The royal standard flying above the palace proclaimed that the King was in residence. Mary thought back to the revels and parties she had attended there in happier times. Often her father had called on her to play the virginal for foreign ambassadors or to dance a galliard with him. He used to call her "the greatest pearl in the kingdom."

The royal barge was moored on the bank of the River Thames below the palace. Mary took the seat of honor in it for the trip upriver. Let them try to move her! She had at least an hour to herself before the rest of the household arrived. Clasping the golden cross that hung around her waist, she prayed for the King, for her mother, and for an end to this troublesome time.

*Her mother dressed Elizabeth in this elaborate gown with its long, trailing skirt for the baby's christening.*

WITHIN A YEAR, Mary's prayers began to be answered. When Anne Boleyn was unable to produce a son, the King's passion for her quickly cooled—then turned to hatred. She was accused of having many other lovers and imprisoned in the grim fortress of the Tower of London. On May 19, 1536, she climbed a scaffold before a crowd of onlookers on Tower Green, and a French swordsman sliced quickly through her elegant white neck.

Although the death of her enemy must have been a relief to Mary, she likely did not rejoice in it. Her own mother had fallen ill and died only four months before. Still living in the household of the young Elizabeth, Mary surely felt some sympathy for her motherless half sister, who was not yet three years old. Eleven days after Anne Boleyn's execution, Henry had married Jane Seymour, a soft-spoken lady of the court only six years older than Mary. Queen Jane wanted to heal the rift between Henry and his eldest daughter, but there was still a major obstacle to be overcome.

*Elizabeth embroidered the cover of this prayer book for her father.*

After the Pope had refused his request for an annulment, Henry had declared himself head of the English church. Mary could not agree with this. She was a devout Roman Catholic who believed that only the Pope could lead the Christian church. Mary also stubbornly refused to agree that the King's marriage to her beloved mother was not genuine. That would mean she was illegitimate, not a princess, just the "accurs'd bastard" Anne Boleyn had once called her.

But after weeks of harsh bullying by court officials, Mary reluctantly signed a document entitled "Lady Mary's Submission." Many prominent people had been beheaded for resisting her father's will. She knew that if she continued to disagree with the King on these matters, she would be sent to the Tower. With her signature, the way was clear for her return to court.

With Mary's rise in the King's favor came a fall in young Elizabeth's fortunes. Since Queen Jane's expected child would become the new heir to the throne, the order of succession had to be changed. When told that she was no longer a princess, Elizabeth, now four, replied, "How haps it, that yesterday I was my Lady Princess and today I am only my Lady Elizabeth?"

When the new royal child—a boy at last—was christened Edward, Prince of Wales, in the chapel of Hampton Court Palace, both Mary and Elizabeth took part in the magnificent ceremony. Elizabeth held the heavy jeweled baptismal robe, and in the procession out of the chapel, took her sister Mary's hand. During the christening, the still-weak Queen Jane lay on a pallet, clasping the King's hand. She developed a high fever the next day and was dead before her son was even two weeks old. In just over a year, three of England's queens had died, and all three of the King's children were motherless.

The role of Elizabeth's mother was filled by her affectionate governess, Katherine "Kat" Champernowne, who would be a trusted companion and servant throughout her life. Kat taught Elizabeth to read fluently, and by the age of six she was beginning to learn Latin. Although the King had always shown affection for the little girl whose russet hair and quick mind were so like his own, Elizabeth was only occasionally summoned to appear in royal ceremonies. For most of the year she lived quietly with a small household of servants at Hatfield or another country manor house.

In 1540, the year Mary turned twenty-four and Elizabeth seven, their father acquired two new wives. The first was the daughter of a Flemish duke, named Anne of Cleves. Henry disliked her on sight, a divorce soon followed, and the official who had arranged the marriage was beheaded. The King's next bride was Katherine Howard, a pretty, young cousin of Anne Boleyn's. But only a year after the wedding, the King discovered that Katherine had other lovers, and so, like her cousin, she was sent to the Tower and then to the scaffold.

Henry VIII's sixth and last wife was a widow named Catherine Parr, whom he married in 1543.

By then, Henry was grossly fat and in poor health, and Catherine was as much a nurse as a wife. She also took a motherly interest in the King's three children and invited Mary, Elizabeth, and Edward to spend more time with their father at court. Catherine found some of the best teachers in England to instruct Elizabeth in Greek, Italian, history, geography, mathematics, and astronomy. One of the tutors later wrote that Elizabeth was "the brightest star" he ever taught. Elizabeth also learned to play the virginal, to her father's delight, and became accomplished at dancing, sewing, and horseback riding. Unlike her brother Edward, however, Elizabeth was never given lessons in the kingly arts of war or politics. She was expected to become the wife of a foreign prince or an English nobleman, nothing more.

But Edward was to become king long before he was ready. On January 27, 1547, Henry lay dying in his canopied bed. Later that day, his nine-year-old son became Edward VI, King of England. Mary and Elizabeth wept when they heard the news. The father they had loved and feared was dead. What, they wondered, would become of his two unmarried daughters?

❧

ON AUGUST 3, 1553, six and a half years after Henry's death, excited crowds clogged the streets of London. At the first sight of the Queen, a tremen-

dous roar went up from the crowd. "Long live our good Queen Mary!" A radiant smile lit up the care-lined face of the small figure seated on a horse covered in golden trappings. Behind the Queen marched more than ten thousand of the men who had rallied to her cause and brought about this triumphal entry into London.

Only two weeks before, in mid-July 1553, Mary had been on the run, pursued by men loyal to the Duke of Northumberland, the Lord Protector of England. During Edward's six-year reign, the Protector and a ruling council had governed for the boy king. When Edward fell ill with tuberculosis in 1552, Northumberland had moved quickly to preserve his power. First, he arranged for his son to marry Lady Jane Grey, a grandniece of Henry VIII. Then he persuaded the sickly Edward to sign a document making Jane first in line to the throne—ahead of Mary and Elizabeth. If Edward died, Jane would become a puppet queen with the powerful Duke pulling all the strings.

But Jane Grey would be queen of England for only nine days. On July 6, 1553, King Edward died at the palace of Greenwich. The Duke of Northumberland kept the sixteen-year-old's death a secret and invited Mary to Greenwich, planning to capture and imprison her. On the way, Mary was warned of the trap and eluded the Duke's men.

*Henry VIII ruled England from 1509 to 1547. He is most remembered for his six wives.*

*The Queen wore a gown of purple velvet . . . all set with goldsmith's work . . . with great pearls on her head.*

A COURTIER, AUGUST 3, 1553

She found refuge in a country castle and called on the help of loyal Catholic friends. But how could one small woman defy the Protector and his army?

Then armed men began arriving at the castle. More men brought horses, weapons, and supplies. Soon the castle walls were surrounded by a huge encampment of almost thirty thousand people. All of them were prepared to fight for their rightful queen. As anger spread at Northumberland's attempt to seize power, his supporters quickly began to desert him. Within days he had surrendered. Now he and his sons were in the Tower, awaiting Mary's judgment.

Another roar from the crowd greeted the appearance of Elizabeth, sitting proudly on her horse, waving her long, tapered fingers. It had been years since she had appeared in public, and people marveled at what a regal and handsome young woman she had become. Now that Mary had prevailed, nineteen-year-old Elizabeth was heir to her

*In her late thirties, Mary was determined to marry and produce an heir to prevent Elizabeth from ever becoming queen.*

throne. But the two sisters represented the two religions that divided England. Mary remained a devout Catholic, determined to return her people to the "true faith." Elizabeth had grown up knowing only the "new faith." During Edward's reign, Protestantism had become the state religion, and Catholicism had been harshly suppressed.

One of the new queen's first tasks was to arrange an official funeral for her brother, Edward. A Protestant service was held in Westminster Abbey, but Mary also ordered a Catholic funeral mass and asked Elizabeth to attend. When Elizabeth refused, Mary was hurt and angry. Memories of her humiliation in Elizabeth's household years before flooded back. The Queen's advisers warned her that her Protestant sister was a danger to her throne.

It soon became obvious to Elizabeth from the snubs she received at court that she had fallen from favor. She asked the Queen if she could leave London and live in the country. Mary consented, as long as Elizabeth studied the Catholic faith and kept a priest in her household.

But Mary hated the thought of the Midnight Crow's daughter, "the darling of the Protestants," succeeding her on the throne. She needed to bear a child and heir. Although only thirty-seven, Mary was past what was considered childbearing age. Various royal husbands were proposed for her. But an ornately framed portrait of Philip, the son of the Emperor of Spain, captured her imagination. As she stared at the youthful face with its intelligent, kind blue eyes, Mary was overcome by emotion. Could a man like this truly be hers? Could this man be both a loving husband and a king who would help her restore her country to the true faith?

The next day her mind was made up. By January 1554, a marriage contract with Spain had been arranged. But cries of, "We will have no foreigner for our king!" were heard in the streets. Spain controlled the most powerful empire in Europe. Would England

*After receiving this painting of Philip, the Emperor of Spain's son, Mary decided she would marry him.*

become just a Spanish colony? And would Protestants be burned at the stake here as they were in Spain? Despite the objections of her council and her people, Mary was firm. It would be Philip or no one.

Only six months after Mary's joyous entry into London, rebellion was brewing in the land. A conspiracy to overthrow the Queen was planned by Sir Thomas Wyatt and other noblemen. Wyatt raised an army of a few thousand men with the call, "Do you want to become slaves of the Spaniards?" As the rebels marched on London, Mary was encouraged to flee the capital. Instead, she courageously rode to the center of London and rallied her people with a moving speech.

Although Wyatt's men managed to enter the city and advance on the Queen's palace, they were finally overcome and arrested. Mary now realized that she had to crush all those who threatened her. The bodies of Wyatt's followers were hung from the gallows throughout the city, and their severed heads were displayed on spikes on gates and bridges.

But Mary's advisers insisted that the biggest threat of all was her sister, Elizabeth. There were accusations that Elizabeth had been aware of the plot and had kept silent. Elizabeth was summoned to Whitehall Palace in London, where she was kept in an isolated room. Elizabeth wrote to Mary protesting her innocence, but the Queen refused to see her. On March 17, 1554, the palace was surrounded by soldiers, and a group of courtiers came to take Elizabeth to the Tower.

As the barge carrying Elizabeth passed under London Bridge, the twisted faces of the rebels' heads mounted there leered down at her. The barge docked at a water entrance to the Tower known as Traitor's Gate. Almost eighteen years before, Elizabeth's mother, Anne Boleyn, had spent her last moments of freedom here. Elizabeth and a few of her ladies were locked in the highest room in the Bell Tower, a cold, damp stone chamber. The next day Mary's officials came to question Elizabeth about her involvement in the rebellion. Elizabeth angrily denied each one of their charges.

On May 19, eighteen years to the day of her mother's execution on Tower Green below, Elizabeth was ordered to be ready to travel. Was this the day Mary would have her beheaded? "This night I think to die," she told her ladies. But Elizabeth was returned to the royal barge and taken down the Thames. Crowds along the bank cheered—much to the Queen's displeasure—when they heard Elizabeth had been released. But her imprisonment was not over. Her new place of confinement was the dark and chilly gatehouse of a run-down country estate near Woodstock. Frequently ill and miserable, Elizabeth appealed to her sister by letter for release.

But the Queen was excitedly awaiting the arrival of her new husband. In mid-July, more than a hundred ships landed in Southampton. A procession of Spanish noblemen, servants, and carts loaded with treasure accompanied the Emperor's son to Winchester, where the royal marriage was to take place. Mary couldn't wait to see him. From the moment Philip entered the candlelit room, he was the portrait come to life. Mary was entranced. To Philip, the small woman in the black velvet dress must have looked more like a spinster aunt than a bride. One of his courtiers said later that Mary was "rather older than we had been told." But Philip kissed Mary on the lips, and the next day they were married in a ceremony filled with royal pomp and splendor.

The next four months were the happiest of Mary's life. She ignored letters from her nuisance of a sister as she showed her adored husband the royal palaces of England. Although many of his men disliked England, and Philip sometimes

*Elizabeth wrote this letter (left) to Mary before she was sent to the Tower (opposite). She drew lines across the second page so that no one could add anything to it.*

seemed homesick, he dutifully performed the role of husband and king. In late November, Philip accompanied the Queen to a service in Westminster Abbey that formally placed the English church under the authority of the Pope. A joyous Mary left the Abbey on her husband's arm. Now all she had to ask of God was a child to inherit her throne and continue His work.

In her freezing rooms at Woodstock, Elizabeth anxiously awaited word from her sister. If she had to spend the winter in this place, she was sure she would die. A message arrived from the court, but not the message she was waiting for: the Queen was expecting a child!

In January 1555, as Mary waited for the birth of her child, the burnings began. To be burned at the stake was the traditional punishment for heresy, defying God's truth. The suppression of Protestant worship was causing dissent throughout the country. Mary believed that for peace to be restored, heresy must be put to the flames. Three Protestant bishops were the first to die in this slow, cruel way. Over the next three years more than three hundred people, including women and children, would be burned to death under Mary's orders.

Many Protestants fled the country. Those that remained looked to Elizabeth as their only hope. As the time for the Queen's delivery drew near, Elizabeth was summoned to Hampton Court to be present at the birth of the royal child. Through June and July, Mary lay in bed looking haggard and old while the country waited for the happy news. By August the doctors had to tell the Queen that there would be no baby. They did not know what had caused the swelling in her stomach, but it was not a child.

A grief-stricken Mary now had to face another

blow. Philip was leaving. He was needed to help govern his father's empire. Mary watched from her window as Philip waved his hat from the departing royal barge. Then she turned away and wept.

IN THE SUMMER of 1558, people pointed up at the brilliant star streaking through the night sky. Comets were believed to foretell the death of kings. Did this mean there would soon be a new sovereign in England? Many hoped this would be so. In the five years of Mary's reign she had brought them under foreign rule by marrying a Spaniard, punished them with heavy taxes, and persecuted them with burnings and executions. The Queen seemed remote, surrounded by priests at her court. And there were rumors that she was ill.

After leaving England, Philip had stayed away for more than a year. When he returned, it was only to ensure that Mary's forces joined the Spanish in a war against France. And he had brought his mistress with him. In January 1558, the English were stunned by news of a crushing defeat in France and the loss of the port of Calais, England's only foothold on the continent. Mary said that when she died, the word "Calais" would be found written on her heart.

Elizabeth had been living quietly at Hatfield, trying to avoid both the Queen's wrath and the foreign husbands she kept proposing for her. During the autumn, as Mary's illness worsened, visitors began coming to Hatfield hoping to find favor with Elizabeth, who might soon be queen. Mary was urged to name Elizabeth her successor.

This was perhaps the bitterest pill of all. Mary made Elizabeth promise to maintain the Catholic Church in England. By now a skilled deceiver,

*At the age of twenty-five, Elizabeth became queen of England.*

Elizabeth agreed. All Mary had worked and prayed for had come to naught. The Midnight Crow's daughter would inherit her throne.

On November 17, 1558, Elizabeth was sitting under one of the large oak trees at Hatfield, reading the Bible. A noise in the distance disturbed her. Turning, she saw a rider dismount and hurry toward her. She recognized one of the Queen's councillors. Through panting breaths he uttered the words "Your Majesty. . . ." Elizabeth fell to her knees and said, "This is the Lord's doing, and it is marvelous in our eyes."

QUEEN ELIZABETH WOULD rule England for the next forty-five years. One of the greatest eras in English history would bear her name—the Elizabethan Age. For her sister there are no memorials anywhere in England. She is remembered only as "Bloody Mary."

# THE FIRST QUEEN ELIZABETH

As a princess, Elizabeth became skilled at avoiding every political trap set for her. After she was crowned, she used those same skills to avoid marriage. A well-educated, clever woman, Elizabeth I encouraged her people to become master mariners, explorers, and traders.

❧ Elizabeth makes Robert Dudley, Earl of Leicester. She once said that if he had been a king's son, she would have married him.

❧ Sir Walter Raleigh begins a colony at Roanoke, Virginia.

 ❧ Elizabeth is crowned.

**1558**

**1564**

❧ William Shakespeare, the playwright and poet, is born.

**1577–80**

❧ Sir Francis Drake sails around the world.

**1584**

**1587**

❧ A Roman Catholic plot to overthrow Elizabeth and put her cousin, Mary, Queen of Scots, on the throne leads to Mary's execution. On her deathbed, Elizabeth made Mary's son, James, her heir.

Mr. WILLIAM
## SHAKESPEARES
COMEDIES,
HISTORIES, &
TRAGEDIES.
Published according to the True Originall Copies.

LONDON
Printed by Isaac Iaggard, and Ed. Blount. 1623.

❧ The Spanish Armada is defeated by the English fleet. King Philip of Spain, who had once been married to her half sister Mary, had failed in his plan to drive Elizabeth from her throne. On hearing the news, a joyous Elizabeth rode her horse up the steps of her hunting lodge.

❧ Sir John Harington invents the flush toilet and installs one for Queen Elizabeth in one of her palaces.

❧ Robert Devereux, 2nd Earl of Essex, a man Elizabeth loved very much, leads a rebellion. The Queen is forced to order his execution for treason.

**1588**   **1591**   **1599**   **1600**   **1601**   **1603**

❧ The Globe Theatre is built. Shakespeare's plays, including *Romeo and Juliet* and *Hamlet*, are produced there.

❧ Elizabeth grants a charter to the East India Company, which controls the silk and spice trade with the Orient.

❧ Elizabeth dies at age seventy.

# THE EMPRESS'S DAUGHTER
## *Marie Antoinette*

TEARS FILLED ANTOINETTE'S pale blue eyes. The Countess of Brandeiss was tying her hair back much too tightly. Antoinette didn't blame her governess, though. It was Mama who expected her to look her best at all times. Not a blond hair could be out of place for the concert that afternoon.

The seven-year-old Archduchess Antoinette liked listening to music, but today she wanted to play outside with her older sister, Caroline. They would soon be leaving Schönbrunn, the Austrian royal family's summer home. Antoinette much preferred this honey-colored palace, with its exotic rooms decorated in the bright colors of faraway India, to the ancient Hofburg Palace in Vienna. She and Caroline spent hours exploring Schönbrunn's gardens or visiting its small private zoo.

But for the next three hours, they would be trapped inside. Antoinette sat down beside her ten-year-old sister in the beautiful Hall of Mirrors. Caroline was fidgeting, as always. Then she screwed up her face and began imitating the squeaky voice of an elderly lady-in-waiting—until her mother sternly swept into the room. Empress Maria Theresa looked like the ruler of a powerful empire. Their father, Emperor Francis, was just the opposite. He winked at them before cheerfully giving the signal for the concert to begin. A six-year-old boy sat down at the harpsichord and immediately caught everyone's attention.

In 1762, Vienna was the music capital of Europe. Stars of the ballet, opera, and symphony regularly visited the city to entertain the Austrian court. The Empress, who had inherited her love of music from her father, made sure that each of her

*Antoinette plays with her dog in the Schönbrunn gardens (opposite).*

*(Above) Antoinette's crest after she becomes queen of France.*

eight daughters and four sons took music lessons. Antoinette played the harp. She could tell that the boy at the harpsichord—Wolfgang Amadeus Mozart—was a much better musician than any of the imperial children, even twenty-one-year-old Joseph, her oldest brother.

"What a little wizard!" Emperor Francis exclaimed. He asked Wolfgang if he could play with the keys covered by a sheet. He could. Could he play with one finger of each hand? He did that, too. Then following his performance, Wolfgang jumped onto the Empress's lap, flung his arms around her plump neck, and kissed her on the cheek!

*Antoinette's sister Maria Christina painted this picture of the imperial family at Schönbrunn. Antoinette is the little girl holding a doll.*

Everyone waited in silence to see what Her Imperial Highness would do. But she just laughed and told her newest discovery to go and play with the other children. As they were all running through a drawing room, Wolfgang slipped and fell on the highly polished floor. The older children laughed, but Antoinette felt sorry for him and helped him up.

"You are kind," he told her. "When I grow up I will marry you."

THREE YEARS LATER, Antoinette needed comforting herself. On August 18, 1765, Emperor Francis died suddenly. In the weeks following his death, Antoinette had long, worried talks with Caroline—sometimes about their gentle father, whom they missed very much—but mostly about Mama.

In her grief, the Empress acted like a different person. She had always worked very hard running the empire. Now she didn't seem to care, and she talked of becoming a nun! On her instructions, all the walls of her rooms had been painted black. She had then told the servants to prepare a coffin for *her* to be placed beside the Emperor's in the royal burial vault.

The Countess of Brandeiss and Madame Weber, Antoinette's old nurse, tried to keep Antoinette's life as normal as possible after her father's death. Growing up in the 2,500-room Hofburg Palace had never, of course, been "normal." More than two thousand servants took care of the palace and its occupants. Before the Emperor died, the royal couple used to hold spectacular dinner parties for ten thousand people at a time!

Now Antoinette sat in her room and wondered if anything exciting would ever happen again. Even the family's cozy theatrical evenings, when the children would sing or play their instruments, had come to an end. And her lessons were incredibly boring. One of her older sisters had once described an archduchess's school day:

*From 8:30 on, penmanship, reading, spelling. Holy Mass at 10:00. French lesson at 11:00. Dinner at noon. Three times a week from 2–3, Fr. Richter [a priest who taught religious studies]. On the other weekdays, this hour for maps, some history, some books and fables. Needlework and the like till 4:00.*

No wonder the Countess of Brandeiss often took pity on Antoinette and cut her lessons short. Once, she had written out her lazy pupil's schoolwork in pencil and let her trace over it in ink.

The Empress called her daughters "sacrifices to politics." Although a brilliant ruler herself, she didn't believe they needed a good education. After all, they wouldn't inherit a crown as she had. They would become the dutiful wives of foreign princes and kings. These men would, in turn, become friends and allies of the Austrian Empire.

In 1768, the King of Spain asked Maria Theresa to pick one of her daughters as a wife for his son, the ugly and dim-witted King of Naples. To Antoinette's horror, fourteen-year-old Caroline was chosen. Knowing her future son-in-law's faults, the Empress wrote, "So long as [Caroline] fulfills her duty toward God and her husband . . . even if she is to be unhappy, I will be pleased."

The new bride was miserable. Their mother had forbidden Caroline to write to Antoinette, probably afraid that gossipy letters would fall into the wrong hands. In 1768, Caroline wrote to her former governess saying how much she missed Antoinette: "When I think her fate may be like mine, I would like to write her entire volumes on the subject." Caroline already knew that her favorite sister had been chosen to marry the heir to the French throne, Louis-Auguste.

France had been Austria's enemy for more than 150 years. But Maria Theresa now believed Prussia and England posed bigger threats to her empire. She signed a treaty with the French king, Louis XV, and offered Antoinette as "the most tender pledge of the happy union between our states. . . ."

AS THE FUTURE queen of France, fourteen-year-old Antoinette quickly became the center of attention at the Austrian court. A French hairdresser fussed over her high forehead, the result of years of pulling her hair back too tightly. A French dentist straightened her crooked teeth. A French dancing instructor taught her how to walk in short little steps, like the women at the royal palace of Versailles. (In their wide hoop skirts, they appeared to float above the marble floors.) And, finally, a patient French tutor tried to help Antoinette make up for the time she had spent ignoring her schoolwork.

For a year, the young teenager wondered what her future husband looked like. Her mother had sent portraits of her daughter to the King of France, but had received none of Louis-Auguste in return. When two finally did arrive, Antoinette hung one of them in her sitting room. The oil painting showed a plain-looking sixteen-year-old boy. She hoped he was more handsome than the portrait suggested.

On April 21, 1770, after an

*Antoinette's brooch, with its portrait of Louis-Auguste.*

exciting, whirlwind month of masked balls and banquets to celebrate her engagement, Antoinette looked around her bedroom in Vienna for the last time. All her traveling clothes for the twenty-three-day trip to France had been loaded onto the coaches, as well as a few precious keepsakes and her little dog. No one familiar—except her French tutor—would be going with her. When Madame Weber appeared at the door, Antoinette ran into her arms. "Dear nurse, I shall love you all my life. Do not forget me!"

Madame Weber and Antoinette walked arm in arm down the long hallway and outside into the bustling courtyard. When she saw her mother waiting with the rest of the family to say good-bye, Antoinette burst into tears. She knew she would probably never see them again. France was too far away. After a last hug, Antoinette climbed into an elegant satin-lined carriage. It had been sent by the King of France to carry the new "dauphine" to meet her fiancé and his family for the first time.

The procession of coaches moved slowly through the old walled city. Fifteen-year-old Antoinette couldn't stop crying, and the stench of manure and garbage on Vienna's narrow streets was—as always—unbearable. She slumped against the red velvet cushions, holding a scented handkerchief to her nose. Then she jumped up suddenly to hang out the window for a final look at her beloved home.

"I SAW A HUGE cortège arriving. It was the King who had the goodness to come and surprise me. As soon as I saw him I threw myself at his feet in great confusion. He took me in his arms, kissing me again and again, calling me his dear daughter," wrote Antoinette in a letter to her mother after meeting Louis XV.

The King was amused by the new dauphine's friendliness and charm. He introduced Marie Antoinette, as she was now known, to his grandson, Louis-Auguste. The awkward sixteen-year-old

*A golden coach carries the new dauphine of France to the palace of Versailles.*

gave the pretty young girl he would be marrying in three days a shy kiss on the cheek. She looked up at him and smiled. Sadly, the portrait hadn't lied. He wasn't the prince of her dreams, but he wasn't a monster either. She felt a little sorry for him.

The Dauphin's parents and grandmother were dead, but other members of the French court stepped forward to meet Marie Antoinette. As the introductions continued, the Comtesse de Noailles sighed heavily. One did not run up to the King of France as though he were a favorite uncle. By ignoring the court's strict etiquette rules, Marie Antoinette made her first enemy at court—her ill-tempered lady-in-waiting.

No one had prepared Marie Antoinette for her new life in a place of "treachery, hatred, and revenge," as one Austrian diplomat described the Versailles court. Unlike Empress Maria Theresa, the spoiled fifty-nine-year-old Louis XV didn't believe his job was to serve his people. He could hunt deer, he could make coffee, and he could take the top off a soft-boiled egg in record-breaking time. That was about it! Meanwhile, his advisers ran the country, although not very well. France was in a state of financial ruin, its overtaxed citizens unhappy.

For the most part, the three thousand aristocrats at the French court served themselves rather than their country. The beautifully dressed nobles and their ladies competed for the most prestigious titles and for various "rights"—for example, the right to live in one of the 226 apartments in the Château de Versailles. They hatched plots and spread lies about their enemies. In the chapel, waiting for the royal wedding to begin, they chattered endlessly about the young bride and groom. One guest wrote:

*The Dauphine was very fine in Diamonds. She is very little and slender. . . . The Dauphin appear'd to have much more timidity than his little Wife. He trembled excessively during the service & blush'd up to his Eyes when he gave the Ring.*

Poor Louis-Auguste. He wanted to be a farmer or a locksmith, not the heir to the French throne. Unfortunately, he had no choice. Louis XV disliked his clumsy grandson, so naturally Louis-Auguste grew up self-conscious and unhappy. And he learned nothing about governing France. Even Madame du Barry, his grandfather's mistress,

called Louis "pudgy and dirty." He tried to forget his troubles by eating huge meals and hunting all day. Even after he married Marie Antoinette, this was how he spent his time.

Faced with a husband who ignored her, the homesick Marie Antoinette turned to Louis-Auguste's unmarried aunts, Adélaïde, Victoire, and Sophie. She visited them every morning and afternoon. The King had cruelly nicknamed his plain, middle-aged daughters "Rag," "Piggy," and "Snip." No one paid much attention to them at court. They spent their days poking their noses into everyone else's business. In drawing the new dauphine into their circle, the jealous sisters saw their chance to play a more important role at the palace and to get back at their father's powerful young mistress, Madame du Barry.

Marie Antoinette played right into their hands. She was confused by the King's relationship with his mistress. After all, her mother had immoral people like du Barry chained to pillars at the city gates! "It is pitiful the weakness he has for Madame du Barry, who is the stupidest and most impertinent creature," she wrote her mother. Marie Antoinette stayed out of the King's way as much as possible and refused to speak to Madame du Barry. This suited the sisters just fine, although it annoyed Louis XV.

Next the cunning aunts offered to take Marie Antoinette's place receiving visitors at court. The gullible teenager thought *mesdames* were simply

*Marie Antoinette plays the harp at Versailles in this official portrait. (Opposite) Miniatures of the royal couple.*

being kind. They knew that holding court did not interest her. Behind Marie Antoinette's back, though, they gleefully told all her secrets and Adélaïde called her *l'Autrichienne*, the Austrian woman. This was a double insult because *chienne* in French means "female dog."

Marie Antoinette's father would have seen right through this meddling threesome. He had once warned his daughter that princesses were "surrounded by a crowd of people who seek only to flatter their taste and to entice them. . . ."

AT THE AUSTRIAN court, the practical Empress had done away with many formal court rituals. But at the French court, Marie Antoinette had to take part in several throughout the day. Something as ordinary as washing her hands in the morning had to be done in the correct French way. And anyone could watch. The immense palace was a public building, and during these "ceremonies," the royal family was on show.

Marie Antoinette couldn't seem to do anything right. She giggled during solemn occasions. When she had nothing to do, she sometimes made fun of people with other young members of the court, just as she and Caroline used to do at home. She tried to hide her smiles and laughter behind a fan, but she still offended many older women from important families.

The loathsome Madame de Noailles corrected

her so many times each day that Marie Antoinette soon began calling her "Madame l'Etiquette." One day Marie Antoinette fell off a donkey in the palace grounds. Servants tried to help her up, but she gaily waved them away. "Leave me on the ground. We must wait for Madame l'Etiquette! She will show us the right way to get up having fallen off a donkey."

Madame de Noailles was just as displeased with the Dauphine's behavior in private. Marie Antoinette's dirty apartment was at the top of her list. Marie Antoinette now had two small dogs and she let them climb up on the expensive furniture in her bedroom, library, and large sitting rooms. The dogs had never been trained, so the servants constantly ran after them, cleaning up their messes. (Marie Antoinette didn't understand why this should be a problem; many of the thousands of people milling about Versailles every day urinated in the hallways because there weren't enough privies.)

Next on the list was the Dauphine's appearance. Marie Antoinette refused to let her ladies-in-waiting tie her into a corset. This lace-trimmed, whalebone-stiffened piece of underwear dug into her ribs. It was indecent not to wear one, complained Madame. Not wearing one will ruin your figure, wrote Mama.

Finally, Marie Antoinette's snubbing of Madame du Barry worried everyone, except Louis-Auguste and his aunts. The King's mistress had powerful friends at court who hated the alliance with Austria. Empress Maria Theresa needed the support of France. She couldn't afford to have her daughter ruffling any feathers. Marie Antoinette bowed to her mother's wishes and spoke—just once—to Madame du Barry. She

looked forward to the day when she would become queen of France and would be able to do or say whatever she liked.

❧

ON A SPRING day in 1773, Marie Antoinette stood on a balcony of the Tuileries Palace in Paris. It overlooked a large formal garden.

"What a crowd!" she exclaimed.

"Madame, here you have two hundred thousand lovers," said the nobleman standing beside her.

Marie Antoinette and Louis-Auguste were taking part in a traditional celebration called the Joyous Entry. Louis XV was growing old and feeble. Before a king died, his heir made the two-hour trip from Versailles to meet his future subjects in Paris.

Thousands had walked through the night from nearby villages to enjoy the festivities. They crowded into the grounds of the Tuileries, hoping to catch a glimpse of the pretty seventeen-year-old princess, in her richly decorated gown, and her nineteen-year-old husband. The young couple seemed to promise a new future for the country.

But could this carefree girl and her clumsy husband successfully rule France when they came to the throne? Her mother was afraid they couldn't. The Empress wrote to her French ambassador, "I count her halcyon [happy] days as over." Sadly, she was right. Just twenty years later, Marie Antoinette stood on a blood-soaked platform and looked across the square at the Tuileries gardens and palace. Below her a very different crowd elbowed and shoved one another, hoping to get a final look at the last queen of France.

# THE LAST QUEEN OF FRANCE

In a time of economic hardship and political upheaval, Marie Antoinette was too young to realize that she had to create a caring, responsible image as queen. The extravagant life she led at Versailles was resented, and soon gossip began to spread about her. Although she never said, "Let them eat cake" when told of a bread shortage, as rumors claimed, she was believed to be an immoral, thoughtless woman.

♣ A second son, Duc de Normandie, is born. He becomes dauphin after his older brother dies in 1789.

♣ A second daughter, Sophie, is born but dies the next year.

♣ Her mother, Empress Maria Theresa, dies.

♣ Louis XVI and Marie Antoinette become king and queen of France.

**1774**  **1778**  **1780**  **1781**  **1785**  **1786**  **1789**

♣ Their first child, Marie Thérèse Charlotte, is born.

♣ The Dauphin, Louis Joseph Xavier, is born.

♣ The French Revolution begins with the July 14 storming of the Bastille, a state prison and symbol of the King's power. This was followed by peasant uprisings throughout France.

♣ On August 26, the National Assembly adopts the Declaration of the Rights of Man and of the Citizen. When the King refuses to approve it, the people of Paris march on Versailles. The royal family is forced to move to Paris.

ARRESTATION DE LOUIS XVI A VARENNES.

🌿 The royal family tries to leave France but is stopped at Varennes and returned to Paris. From then on, they are considered traitors.

🌿 Marie Antoinette is led to her execution (above) and guillotined (below) on October 16. She is only 38. Louis XVI had been put to death on January 21.

🌿 Marie Antoinette's ten-year-old son, Louis XVII, dies in prison, but her seventeen-year-old daughter (below) is freed and lives in exile for much of her life.

**1790**   **1791**   **1792**   **1793**   **1795**

🌿 The aristocracy is abolished.

🌿 The royal family is imprisoned in the Temple Prison. France is proclaimed a republic.

# "I WILL BE GOOD"
## *Victoria*

VICTORIA LOOKED UP at the sign, then nodded happily to her future subjects. She had never seen her name written in pink bows and flowers before! An enthusiastic crowd greeted Victoria on her trip to Wales in 1832. They seemed just as pleased with the tiny thirteen-year-old princess as she was with them. "What a relief," they said to one another. "She looks like a normal lass. A little short, but normal."

Three very odd kings had ruled England over the previous seventy years. Victoria's grandfather, George III, had been insane. Her enormously fat uncle, George IV, deserted his wife, Queen Caroline, and stripped away her title. And the new king, the boorish William IV, was said to be as "cracked" as his father. Everyone looked forward to the day Victoria would become queen.

Victoria herself found the idea terrifying. She remembered the day she had discovered her destiny. It had been two years earlier. Poor King George was dying. Louise Lehzen, Victoria's governess, had slipped the royal family tree into a history book Victoria was reading. And there it was! No children's names appeared after George IV or his brother, William. As their niece, Victoria was next in the line of succession.

"I see I am nearer to the Throne than I thought," she had said shakily. And then when the enormity of it all had hit her, she had taken Lehzen's bony hand in her own and said very solemnly, "I will be good."

Even though she was a member of the royal family, Victoria hadn't been raised, like Marie Antoinette, in a splendid palace fit for a future queen. Her father, Edward, the Duke of

*Victoria stares out the window at Kensington Palace (opposite).*

*(Above) Victoria's coat of arms.*

*(Above) Kensington Palace, Victoria's birthplace. Her sketch of her governess,
Lehzen (opposite, above) and some of her dolls (opposite, below).*

Kent, had died when she was a baby. He had left his German-speaking wife almost penniless.

The eight-month-old Victoria and her mother, the Duchess of Kent, were allowed to stay in their sparsely furnished apartment in Kensington Palace on the outskirts of London. Féodore, the Duchess's twelve-year-old daughter from her first marriage, lived with them. An eccentric duke, a disgraced princess, and several other poor "royals" also shared the run-down mansion.

The Duchess of Kent received a small income from the government and some money from her brother, Prince Leopold. But she didn't think it was enough to raise a future queen like Victoria. Teachers, ladies-in-waiting, a governess, maids, footmen—they all cost money. She turned for help to John Conroy, a good-looking former soldier who had served her husband, the Duke. He quickly agreed to take charge of the Duchess's finances.

But Conroy had a plan of his own. He would make Victoria and her mother completely dependent on him. Both "Uncle Kings" might die before their niece's eighteenth birthday. If this happened, Victoria would need an adult to help her rule.

With the Duchess as regent and himself as her right-hand man, John Conroy would be in a *very* powerful position at court.

THE DUCHESS OF KENT often read her daughter's diary, so Victoria never described John Conroy in it. If she had, she would probably have called him "detestable." She hated him with a passion—and with good reason.

By the time Victoria was eight, Conroy was striding about the apartment, shouting out orders. "I was always crushed and kept under and hardly dared say a word," she remembered later. If she did misbehave, she had to stand on a dark stair-landing with her hands tied behind her back.

Conroy's first step in his plan to control the Duchess of Kent's household was to keep Victoria away from the King. Conroy didn't want anyone else giving advice to the future queen or her mother. He told the Duchess that the royal family planned to kidnap the Princess and raise her themselves. Because the Duchess had never been treated well by the royal family, she believed him.

From then on, Victoria was never left alone. Someone always held her hand as she walked down the dim, winding stairs connecting the two floors of the family's apartment. She always slept in her mother's bedroom. Conroy even provided Victoria with a friend the same age—his own daughter, and spy, Victoire. Although she never liked "Miss V. Conroy," as she called her in her diary, Victoria was forced to play with her.

When the people she loved began leaving Kensington Palace, Victoria panicked. Imagine having only Mama, John Conroy, and Victoire for company—it was a frightening thought! In 1828, her half sister, Féodore, married Prince Ernest of Hohenlohe-Langenburg. Féodore didn't love him, but marriage offered her an escape from the dreadful Sir John Conroy (he had already managed to garner a title for himself).

The middle-aged Baroness Späth left soon afterward. The Duchess's kind, homely lady-in-waiting had always been a part of their lives.

Victoria may have seen Sir John flirting with the Duchess and told Späth about it. Then the Baroness probably spoke out against Conroy to her mistress. She was soon fired, supposedly for "spoiling" the Princess.

Victoria sometimes heard her mother arguing with Conroy. But the Duchess obviously couldn't win an argument with this determined man. After all, she had just dismissed a loyal friend of twenty-five years. Would "dear good Lehzen" be next? Victoria clung to her slim, dark-haired governess, her last true friend.

Lehzen helped her pupil forget about the tense atmosphere at home by escaping into an imaginary world. The two of them made tiny gowns and costumes for 132 dolls. Each doll had a name and a made-up family history. As Victoria began going to the opera and ballet, she dressed half the dolls in her collection as performers she had seen on stage.

It was hard not to notice, though, that Conroy treated Louise Lehzen unkindly. The way he

*(Left) Victoria's mother, the Duchess of Kent, wearing one of her elaborate hats. (Right) Sir John Conroy.*

teased Victoria about her own appearance was bad enough. (He said she looked like her stupid cousin, "Silly Billy," the Duke of Gloucester.) But Victoria hated the way Conroy made rude comments about Lehzen, even over trivial things like sprinkling caraway seeds on her food. Fortunately, Victoria's governess was clever enough not to challenge Conroy as Späth had done. But Victoria never got over her fear that Lehzen, too, would be dismissed.

AS HER DAUGHTER entered her teens, the Duchess turned into an unbearable snob. She began wearing rich velvet gowns, strings of pearls, and enormous hats perched on her chestnut-colored hair. Conroy encouraged "the mother of the future queen" to demand renovations to her Kensington apartment. Then she demanded new furniture. Her frequent, shrill requests annoyed the aging William IV, as did her rudeness to his wife, Queen Adelaide, and her "royal" trips around the countryside with Victoria. Nonetheless, the King and Queen never included Victoria in their dislike of her mother.

On May 24, 1833, the royal couple gave Victoria a juvenile ball at St. James's Palace. A night out with other young people, particularly boys, was the perfect gift for Victoria's fourteenth birthday. It certainly beat Mama's gifts, which were recorded in the Princess's diary: "a lovely bag of her own work [made by the Duchess], a beautiful bracelet . . . two dresses, some prints, some books, some handkerchiefs, and an apron." Victoria "danced in all 8 quadrilles," then sat in the place of honor between her aunt and uncle at supper. The

# To-day is my birthday. I am to-day fourteen years old! How very old!

VICTORIA, MAY 24, 1833

next day she wrote, "We came home at half past 12. I was *very* much amused."

During the next two years, the friction between Kensington and the royal family grew. Victoria felt caught in the middle—"between two fires." She knew she was being used by Sir John and her mother, and she began to rebel in little ways. When she saw Sir John, Victoria fixed him with a stony gaze. The Duchess always scolded her for saying anything nice about the King and Queen. And so, after a visit to Windsor Castle, she wrote in her journal, "I was very pleased there, as both my Uncle and Aunt are so very kind to me." She knew that the Duchess would read it and disapprove.

Victoria's first great battle with Sir John and her mother took place in October 1835. And her little white bed was the battlefield.

*Victoria owned a pony, a canary, and a parakeet, but her King Charles spaniel quickly became her favorite pet.*

DASH MOPED AT the foot of the bed. Victoria's black King Charles spaniel was the only good thing Sir John had ever brought into her life. And he hadn't really given "Dear Dashy" to her but to her mother. Victoria half remembered a line from her favorite writer, Walter Scott. Something about dogs being "companions" and "incapable of deceit." Dash had certainly become her best friend in the world.

At sixteen, however, Victoria didn't feel as alone as she once had. She still had Lehzen—thank goodness—and the King and Queen and Baron Stockmar (an old family friend) and Uncle Leopold. She thought of her uncle as the father she'd never had. He gave her advice on her future life as a monarch and suggested books to read. The previous year, she had written him what he had called "a very clever, sharp little letter." She had said, "I am much obliged to you, dear Uncle, for the extract about Queen Anne, but must beg you, as you have sent me to show what a Queen *ought not* to be, that you will send me what a Queen *ought* to be."

But now it was difficult to find anything to smile about. Her body felt like it was on fire. She dimly remembered the doctor leaning over her. The Duchess and Conroy had waited an entire

week before calling him. Anytime Victoria had a headache or felt sick, they would say it was just a whim. They liked people to think Victoria was a foolish, stupid little girl who imagined all sorts of things and would always need their guidance. But when she became delirious, they had had to admit something was seriously wrong.

Victoria had typhoid, an illness that was often fatal. She stayed in bed for more than a month. When she finally looked into her silver hand mirror, Victoria shuddered. She hadn't been able to sleep or eat. Her blue eyes, which bulged a little at the best of times, seemed to be popping out of her head. She had lost a lot of weight, and her usually thick, shiny hair had begun to fall out. Lehzen sadly suggested they should cut it until it grew in again. In the 1800s a girl's hair was her "crowning glory." To be "literally now getting *bald*," as Victoria wrote in her diary, was appalling. But the worst was yet to come.

King William, although over seventy, seemed likely to live past Victoria's eighteenth birthday. This made Conroy very nervous. The Duchess might never become regent. When Victoria came to the throne, the government would give her a

Her Accession.

*On June 20, 1837, Victoria was told that her uncle had died during the night and she was now queen.*

huge fortune to pay her hundreds of servants and to run her palaces. Conroy desperately wanted control of that money.

Knowing that Victoria was weak and vulnerable, he barged into her sickroom and demanded she sign a document. The document would have guaranteed that he would be made her private secretary when she became queen. But with Lehzen at her side to give her courage, and remembering her Uncle Leopold's support, Victoria refused to sign anything.

Conroy stormed out of the room and called the Duchess in to make her daughter obey. Victoria listened as her mother tried to persuade her. All the while, Sir John was shouting at Lehzen. Victoria found it hard to believe that her own mother would be a part of this bullying. Over and over again, she refused to sign the document.

When Victoria got better, she hardly spoke to her mother and didn't say a word to Conroy. She never again visited his family in their house next door. A much stronger and more confident Victoria knew that it wouldn't be long now before the English crown passed to her.

FINALLY, VICTORIA TURNED eighteen on May 24, 1837. Conroy and his puppet, the Duchess, were still trying to seize control. But Victoria's friends gave her great support. "Be steady, my good child," wrote Uncle Leopold, ". . . as long as I live [I will be] a faithful friend and supporter." Baron Stockmar wrote Leopold, "The Princess continues to refuse firmly to give her Mamma her promise that she will make O'Hum [the Baron's nickname for Conroy] her confidential adviser. Whether she will hold out, Heaven only knows, for they plague her, every hour and every day."

Because the Princess had led such a secluded life, no one in the government really knew what she was like. As the King now lay dying, this concerned them. Was Victoria as dim-witted and unhealthy as they had been led to believe by Conroy and the Duchess?

On June 15, Lord Liverpool visited Kensington. Conroy told him that Victoria was "younger in intellect than in years." She would never be able to cope as queen without him as private secretary. Baron Stockmar, however, had insisted that Lord Liverpool see Victoria alone. The Princess soon told him about the "many slights and incivilities" she had put up with from Conroy. This "rendered it totally impossible for her to place him in any confidential situation," Lord Liverpool wrote afterward. Victoria's assured, intelligent manner won him over completely.

Victoria also faced the future knowing that she wouldn't rule alone. Although she was forced to choose a future husband from a small group of royal cousins, at least she had a choice. The fact that her mother thought her German cousin, Albert of Saxe-Coburg and Gotha, would make an excellent husband only made her determined to dislike him. But after meeting him, she wrote in her diary that he was "extremely handsome," "clever," and "very very merry." Her Uncle Leopold liked Albert, and Victoria decided he "possessed every quality that could be desired to render me perfectly happy." He even liked Dashy.

On June 19, 1837, King William died. Victoria's mother woke her up at six the next morning. "I got out of bed and went into my sitting-room (only in my dressing-gown) and *alone*, and saw them [the Archbishop of Canterbury and Lord Conyngham]. Lord Conyngham then acquainted me that my poor Uncle, the King, was no more . . . and consequently that I am Queen. [He] knelt down and kissed my hand. . . ."

Victoria ruled as queen of Great Britain for more than sixty years. She married Prince Albert and they had nine children, who married into many of the royal families of Europe. Like Elizabeth I, she gave her name to an era—the Victorian Age.

*(Above and right) Miniature portraits of the royal couple.*

# VICTORIA AS QUEEN

The little princess who had promised to be "good" became a strong-willed, conscientious queen. During her reign, the British Empire grew to cover nearly one quarter of the world's land surface. A loving wife and mother, she was held up as a model of the Victorian ideal of decency and respectability.

♧ Victoria and Prince Albert are married in February. Their first child, Victoria ("Vicky"), is born in November.

♧ The Queen's image appears on the world's first adhesive postage stamp, the penny black.

♧ Victoria opens the Great Exhibition, the first world's fair. Its huge glass and iron Crystal Palace (left) showcases the new machines invented during the Industrial Revolution.

♧ The Great Potato Famine begins in Ireland, killing more than one million people by 1849.

**1838**  **1840**  **1842**  **1845**  **1850**  **1851**

♧ Charles Dickens publishes *Oliver Twist*, one of his most famous books.

♧ Victoria is crowned.

♧ Children under the age of ten are forbidden to work underground in mines.

♧ Victoria arranges for the care of a young African princess rescued by a British naval commander during a mission to Africa to help end the slave trade. Sarah Forbes Bonetta remained a friend of the royal family throughout her life. Her daughter, Victoria, was the Queen's godchild.

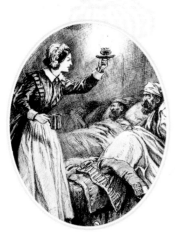

🍀 The Crimean War breaks out between Russia and Britain, France, and Ottoman Turkey. Victoria presents the first Victoria Crosses (below), awarded for bravery in the face of the enemy. Florence Nightingale (above) travels to the Crimea to care for the wounded. Victoria supported the efforts of this brave nurse, who revolutionized the nursing profession.

🍀 *Alice's Adventures in Wonderland* by Lewis Carroll is published.

🍀 Victoria's first great-grandchild is born.

🍀 Victoria's Golden Jubilee.

🍀 Women at a match factory go on strike to protest against unsafe working conditions, long hours, and low wages. They form the Matchgirls' Union, inspiring other unskilled workers to form trade unions.

🍀 Free primary-school education becomes available to all children in England.

| 1854~56 | 1861 | 1865 | 1879 | 1887 | 1888 | 1897 | 1899 | 1901 |

🍀 Victoria's mother, the Duchess of Kent, dies in March. (After Vicky's birth, Victoria and her mother had become close again.) Prince Albert, age forty-two, dies of typhoid fever in December. Victoria remains in mourning for the rest of her life, making few public appearances.

Victoria's Diamond Jubilee marked the sixtieth anniversary of her reign.

🍀 Queen Victoria dies at age eighty-two. At her death, she has thirty-seven great-grandchildren.

*The Queen and some of her family in 1896.*

# THE ISLAND ROSE

## *Ka'iulani*

HE ELEVEN-YEAR-OLD princess traced the amazing journey of her two aunts across the map of the world. They had set sail from Honolulu, crossed the United States, sailed from New York, and landed in London—a long way to travel in 1887. But who could ignore an invitation to Queen Victoria's Golden Jubilee celebrations? Ka'iulani (ka-ee-oo-LAH-nee) imagined herself in their place, meeting and congratulating the ruler of the British Empire at Buckingham Palace.

Queen Victoria had always been her role model. Victoria Ka'iulani, Kalaninuiahilapalapa Kawēkiu i Lunalilo Cleghorn would rule her own country one day. She hoped her reign would be as successful as her namesake's had been. If only her mother had not said those terrifying things. . . .

On her deathbed, Princess Miriam Likelike whispered to Ka'iulani: "I have seen your future very plainly. You will go far away for a very long time. You will never marry. And you will never be queen." Shortly afterward, she died. That had only been a few months earlier. Ka'iulani's governess had made her feel a bit better by telling her that dying people often said things that weren't true.

That year Ka'iulani spent even more time than usual riding Fairie, her white pony. They rode out to the famous cape called Diamond Head or around the family's lush estate on Waikiki Beach. She and her Scottish-born father, Archie Cleghorn, lived there alone now. It made Ka'iulani sad to smell the white gardenias her father had planted for Mama. When gloomy thoughts pushed their way into her mind, she went surfing or had a "sea bath" with a friend or played with her peacocks. Ka'iulani

*Ka'iulani (opposite) surrounded by her favorite flower—the pikake—with Diamond Head in the background.*

*(Above) The Hawai'ian flag.*

remembered her mother fondly but tried to forget what she had said.

⤙⤚

*Forth from her land to mine she goes,*
*The island maid, the island rose,*
*Light of heart and bright of face,*
*The daughter of a double race.*
ROBERT LOUIS STEVENSON, WRITTEN IN
KA'IULANI'S AUTOGRAPH BOOK, 1888

WHILE KA'IULANI'S TWO AUNTS, Queen Kapi'olani and Princess Lili'uokalani, celebrated Victoria's fiftieth anniversary as queen, their own monarch was in trouble. A group of mostly American businessmen and sugar-plantation owners had formed the Hawai'ian League. Its aim was to control Hawai'i economically as well as politically. It forced King Kalākaua, who owed the league a lot of money, to appoint a new cabinet made up of its members. Then they ordered him to sign a new constitution. In it, the king's powers were greatly reduced. The humiliated Kalākaua and many of his people felt their island nation was being taken from them.

During this unhappy time, Ka'iulani met the famous author of *The Strange Case of Dr. Jekyll and Mr. Hyde* and *Treasure Island*. On his visit to Hawai'i, Robert Louis Stevenson became friends with the royal family. The tall, thin writer first met Ka'iulani under her favorite tree on the beautiful estate—a banyan tree. They talked about the book she was reading and walked up to the house together to see her father. Mr. Stevenson captivated the thirteen-year-old with stories about his travels around the world. He also made Ka'iulani feel more excited and less afraid about her own trip abroad.

The royal family knew the Crown Princess would have to be well educated to fight the foreigners, or *haoles* (HOW-lees), in the future. They decided to send her to Britain, Hawai'i's old ally and her father's native land, to continue her studies. The first part of her mother's odd prophecy seemed to be coming true! With tears in her eyes, Ka'iulani made the King promise she would only be gone for a year.

In 1889, Ka'iulani arrived in England and became a student at Great Harrowden Hall, a girls' school outside London. A year stretched into two years. At home, the

*Ka'iulani's aunts, Queen Kapi'olani (left) and Princess Lili'uokalani (right) dressed for Queen Victoria's Golden Jubilee.*

*Ka'iulani (first row, center) and her friends wear leis around their necks at a luau, a traditional Hawai'ian party.*

King died and her aunt became queen. On the day Ka'iulani heard the sad news, she wrote to Her Majesty Queen Lili'uokalani, "I little thought when I said goodbye to my dear Uncle nearly two years ago that it would be the last time I should see his dear face." As the Crown Princess, surely she would now be asked to return to her beloved islands.

Two years later she was still living in England. The summer before her seventeenth birthday, Ka'iulani finally received the news she had been waiting for. She would return to Hawai'i for her eighteenth birthday. "I am having such very pretty summer dresses made," she wrote to her aunt. "I do like pretty, dainty things. All the ladies are wearing dresses made like men's clothes. I do dislike them so, they look so manly."

The summer flew by. Ka'iulani helped raise money for charity and began to plan her tour of Europe, a trip all proper young society ladies took. Most exciting of all, a date had been set for her to be presented to Queen Victoria.

On January 30, 1893, three telegrams arrived. Two words in them broke Ka'iulani's heart: "Queen Deposed." Queen Lili'uokalani had wanted to replace the "Bayonet Constitution" with one that restored the ruler's powers and gave the right to vote to more native Hawai'ians. But before she could do so, her government was overthrown by a group of *haoles* who wanted Hawai'i to join the United States. A proclamation was read, setting up a temporary government "until terms of union with the United States of America have been negotiated and agreed upon."

The U.S. Minister in Hawai'i favored annexation, which would make the islands part of his country. He believed the Americans who had taken over the government and others who lived on the eight islands needed his protection. He ordered troops on a U.S. ship in the harbor to land in Honolulu. The Queen, not wanting to see the lives of Hawai'i's men endangered, surrendered under protest to "the superior force of the United States of America."

IN FEBRUARY 1893, Ka'iulani sailed to New York on the *Teutonic* with the Davies family. Theo Davies, a former British consul to Hawai'i, had been her guardian while she was in Britain. He

*A portrait of Princess Ka'iulani taken in England before her return to Hawai'i.*

had advised her to go as quickly as she could to Washington to persuade President Grover Cleveland to reject the Annexation Treaty and to restore her aunt to power. Ka'iulani doubted that anybody would listen to a seventeen-year-old girl. But then she remembered that Queen Victoria had been only eighteen when she came to the throne. She had to do her best to save her country.

On the busy New York pier, the Princess spoke to the large crowd of reporters awaiting her arrival: "Today I, a poor, weak girl, with not one of my people near me and all of these statesmen against me, have the strength to stand up for the rights of my people. Even now I can hear their wail in my heart, and it gives me strength and I am strong. . . ." One magazine writer described her as "a dignified young woman: tall, slight, straight." Certainly, her beauty attracted attention wherever she went. But many Americans also listened to her intelligent pleas for their support.

The following month Ka'iulani received an invitation to the White House. The President had withdrawn the Annexation Treaty. In the Blue Room, the portly American leader reassured his beautiful guest that matters would be put right in her country. After her triumphant trip, Ka'iulani returned to England, still a princess in a foreign land but a very happy one.

PRINCESS KA'IULANI FINALLY returned to Hawai'i in 1897, eight years after she had been sent away to school. She never married. When her aunt suggested possible husbands, she said, "I feel it would be wrong if I married a man I did not love." And she never became queen. In 1897, with a new president in power, the Annexation Treaty was reintroduced to Congress and passed, making Hawai'i a part of the United States. Ka'iulani kept fighting for the rights of native Hawai'ians until her death.

Unwell for years with heart disease, the Crown Princess of Hawai'i died in her own bedroom on the royal estate in Hawai'i in 1899. She was only twenty-four. Some say that at the very instant she died, Ka'iulani's pet peacocks all began to screech in an eerie death wail that could be heard miles away.

*Ka'iulani (far right) feeds her peacocks in one of the last photographs taken of her.*

# THE TSAR'S DAUGHTERS
## Olga, Tatiana, Marie, and Anastasia Nikolayevna

A SHAFT OF SUNLIGHT suddenly lit up the ornate dome of the cathedral. Anastasia looked up and saw two birds circling there, high above the clouds of incense rising from the golden altar. She nudged her older sister Marie, who gave her a sharp jab back as if to say, "Schwibs, don't you dare make me laugh!"

Their mother would be furious if the Tsar's daughters had a fit of the giggles. Especially in front of all of St. Petersburg society. Especially during a solemn choral mass in honor of the three hundred years that the Romanov family had ruled Russia. Earlier on that morning of March 6, 1913, all heads had turned as the four girls entered the cathedral in their white silk dresses with scarlet sashes. The Tsar's daughters weren't seen in public very often. They could almost hear the thoughts of the capital's grand ladies: "My, my, the two older girls are quite grown-up. The second one, Tatiana, is that her name? She's a beauty. The two younger girls look a little chubby. And the Tsarevich, the son and heir, what's wrong with him? He had to be carried into the church. Does the future of the Romanov dynasty rest on his frail little shoulders?"

Tsarina Alexandra was all too aware of the beady eyes gazing upon her family. She hated this gossipy world and kept her children away from it as much as she could. For most of the year, her family lived in the country outside St. Petersburg in the secluded compound of Tsarskoe Selo ("the Tsar's village"). There, behind high iron railings, stood two splendid palaces surrounded by eight hundred acres of groomed lawns and gardens with fountains, an artificial lake, and an imitation Chinese

*(Opposite, left to right) Marie, Anastasia, Olga, and (seated) Tatiana.*

*(Top) A brooch made by the famous jeweler, Fabergé, in honor of the Romanovs' three hundredth anniversary. (Above) A watercolor by Anastasia.*

village. For their home, the Tsarina had chosen the "small" Alexander Palace (with only one hundred rooms) and had decorated the family wing with bright patterns and cozy furniture. The massive blue-and-gold Catherine Palace nearby was used only for formal occasions.

Outside Tsarskoe Selo, armed horsemen circled day and night guarding Tsar Nicholas and his family. Many Russians had become impatient with the absolute rule of the Tsar, and some of them were prepared to use violence to bring about political change. In most other European countries, ruling monarchs had given over much of their power to elected politicians. But Russia, the largest country in the world, was behind the times. Eighty percent of its people were uneducated peasants who toiled in fields owned by wealthy landowners. Large factories in Russian cities paid their workers poor wages, which forced them to live in miserable slums.

Nicholas believed that most Russians were simple, religious people who needed the firm hand of a father figure. He intended to rule as his ancestors had for the previous three hundred years. But eight years earlier, strikes, riots, and rebellion had broken out across the country. Nicholas had been forced to grant Russia a constitution and allow an elected parliament called the Duma. Nicholas found these changes hard to accept.

But even harder for him had been the discovery that his infant son, Alexei, had a serious

*Fabergé created the world's most fabulous Easter eggs for the Tsar's family. This one from 1913 shows Nicholas and his ancestors.*

disease called hemophilia. In late September 1904, when he was only six weeks old, the baby Tsarevich had bled from his navel. Alexandra had grown very afraid, for she recognized the symptoms of this disease—her brother and her uncle had both died from it. A hemophiliac's blood does not clot properly, which means that any bruise or fall can cause serious internal bleeding—and death. Alexandra's grandmother, Queen Victoria, was an unknowing carrier of the gene that causes hemophilia. From her it was passed on through her daughters and granddaughters to the sons of the European royals they married.

Alexandra suffered terribly whenever her son had a bout of severe bleeding. At the three hundredth anniversary mass in the cathedral, Alexei was still recovering from an attack that had brought him close to death. In October 1912, the eight-year-old had banged his leg on the side of a bathtub. During the family's visit to the Tsar's hunting lodge, the injury had suddenly grown worse. For ten days Alexei lay in bed moaning while blood flowed into his upper leg and abdomen. His mother never left his bedside. When death seemed near, a priest was summoned to conduct the last rites. Then a telegram arrived. It was from the person Alexandra always turned to in times of great need. It said, "God has seen your tears and heard your prayers. Do not grieve. The Little One will not die."

Within hours Alexei's bleeding had stopped. The sender of the telegram was a tall, bearded peasant from Siberia named Grigory Rasputin. He called himself a *starets*, a wandering holy man. Many people in St. Petersburg called him a fraud and a drunk. But to Alexandra he was a gift from God. When Rasputin prayed or laid his hands on Alexei, the Tsarevich's bleeding would miraculously stop. Since Alexei's hemophilia had to be kept a secret, people wondered why a coarse peasant like Rasputin visited the palace so often. How could the Tsarina allow that dreadful man into her home?

But Olga, Tatiana, Marie, and Anastasia admired Rasputin and called him by their special family name, "Our Friend." If Our Friend could stop Alexei's painful bleeding, then he must truly be a man of God. The girls doted on their brother and never seemed to resent all the extra attention he received. They knew he was the heir to the throne and that their role was to protect him.

The four sisters were so close they sometimes signed OTMA—the first letter of their names—on letters and cards. Throughout their childhood their mother dressed them in identical clothes. She called Olga and Tatiana the "Big Pair" and Marie and Anastasia the "Little Pair."

In March 1913, the "Big Pair" were seventeen and fifteen. The tall, classically beautiful Tatiana was their mother's favorite. The others called her

*In this formal portrait taken with their brother, Alexei, the sisters wear white silk dresses and pearl Russian-style tiaras.*

"the Governor" because she was a little bossy. Although Olga was older, she was quiet and serious and spent much of her time reading. She often rebelled against her mother's rules by becoming withdrawn and sulky. Though plump, thirteen-year-old Marie had a face "like an angel," with beautiful large eyes "like saucers." Known as "Mashka," she was warm and playful and wanted to grow up and marry a Russian soldier and have twenty children. Eleven-year-old Anastasia was the other half of the "Little Pair." Stories of her jokes and pranks had already become family legend. She could make her father double over with her imitation of the waddle of a particularly fat lady-in-waiting. Her nickname was "Schwibsik," which means "imp" in Russian.

The Tsar's daughters turned heads once again in May at a three hundredth anniversary parade in Moscow's Red Square. And on a boat trip up the Volga River, crowds of peasants had waded into the water to get a closer glimpse of the imperial family, shouting out "God save the Tsar!" For the Tsarina, this was all the proof she needed that her husband's ministers were only trying to frighten them with their talk of revolution. "You see it yourself," she remarked. "We need merely to show ourselves and at once their hearts are ours."

*Tatiana (left) and her sisters dance with the officers on the* Standart *in July 1912.*

THE GLEAMING BLACK *Standart* was the most splendid royal yacht in the world. It had comfortable staterooms, servants' quarters, a chapel, and even its own musicians. Every summer the imperial family enjoyed carefree days on board as they cruised through the islands off the coast of Finland. The girls enjoyed flirting with the yacht's young officers, who looked so handsome in their white summer uniforms. "I terribly want to dance and wait for an hour to come when I will dance with the officers," wrote Anastasia from the yacht one summer.

It was on board the *Standart*, in June 1914, that the Tsar was informed of the assassination of the heir to the throne of the Austro-Hungarian Empire. He did not know then that this single event would plunge all of Europe into war. But Alexandra had some sense of the coming catastrophe. Rasputin had been sending her letters warning that "a terrible storm cloud hangs over Russia."

On the night of August 1, 1914, the Tsar arrived home looking pale and shaken. When he told Alexandra that war had just been declared, she fled from the room in tears. Later she confided to a lady-in-waiting, "War! This is the end of everything!"

Before her marriage, Alexandra had been a German princess. Now her homeland was the enemy. But Alexandra was determined to show her husband's people that she was a true Russian. She and Olga and Tatiana trained as nurses and worked long hours tending wounded soldiers. She even set up a hospital on the grounds of Tsarskoe Selo, which the "Little Pair" regularly visited. "Today we went to the large palace infirmary," Marie wrote to her father. "Mama, Olga, and Tatiana went to do the bandaging. Alexei and I went through the wards and talked to every soldier."

In the summer of 1915, Nicholas decided to take command of the army himself and spent most of his time at military headquarters in western Russia. At home, Alexandra became more involved in running the government. Every day she would write to the Tsar, giving him advice that had usually come from Rasputin. "Hearken to Our Friend" she wrote, "he has your interest and Russia's at heart—it is not for nothing that God sent him to us." Wild rumors began to circulate that the Tsarina—and the government—were under the control of an ignorant peasant. Some claimed Alexandra and Rasputin were spies for Germany. At the front, millions of Russians were being slaughtered. At home their families were going hungry. Why couldn't the Tsar do something?

Two young relatives of the Tsar decided to take matters into their own hands in December 1916. They lured Rasputin to a party, shot him, and shoved his body under the ice of the Neva River. The Tsarina was devastated. She ordered that Rasputin be buried at Tsarskoe Selo. Before his death it is claimed that he wrote a chilling letter to the Tsar that said, ". . . if it was your relations who have wrought my death then no one of your family will remain alive for more than two years. They will all be killed by the Russian people."

THE TSAR'S TRAIN had still not returned to Tsarskoe Selo. "But the train is *never* late," wailed Anastasia. "Oh, if Papa would only come quickly." During the night of March 13, 1917, soldiers loyal to the Tsar had surrounded the Alexander Palace to protect it from unruly mobs. Alexandra knew the situation was serious. Olga, Tatiana, and Alexei were in bed with the measles. Marie and Anastasia had been trying to help their mother but were both starting to feel sick. "Please don't let me be ill," Anastasia kept repeating. "Everything will be all right when Papa comes home."

But Nicholas did not come home until more than a week later. And when he did, he was no longer the tsar of Russia. Rioting in the capital had turned into outright rebellion. A group of army generals had urged Nicholas to give up his throne for the good of the country. Reluctantly, he had signed the Order of Abdication. Members of the Duma had formed a provisional government. "How different everything is," Nicholas wrote in his diary on the day of his return to Tsarskoe Selo. "The street and the park around the palace are full of sentinels [guards]. . . ."

The man who had ruled over one-sixth of the globe was now a prisoner in his own palace. For a while, the family's life resumed some of its normal routine. Alexei and the "Little Pair" continued lessons with their tutors in the schoolroom. Olga kept her nose in a book and Tatiana practiced the piano. In the afternoon they were allowed walks on the grounds, although they avoided going near the gates where people gathered to stare at them. When spring came they decided to dig a vegetable garden. The Tsarina watched and knitted while the girls carried away sod and wheeled a huge water barrel for their newly planted seeds.

In August they learned they would have to leave Tsarskoe Selo. Early on the morning of August 14, 1917, they boarded a train bound for Siberia. That evening Nicholas wrote in his diary, "The sunrise that saw us off was beautiful. . . . Thank God we are saved and together."

FOR FOUR MONTHS the former imperial family had been living under guard in a large white house in the town of Tobolsk, Siberia. The four girls shared a room and decorated it with photographs of the *Standart* and of other happy times. Their father chopped and stacked wood in the yard. The girls read, wrote in their diaries, and embroidered. Sometimes they put on plays for the family's amusement.

"Today passed just as yesterday. . . . It is boring," wrote Alexei in his diary. In April 1918 he decided to relieve the tedium by sliding his sled down the inside stairs. He fell off, which brought on a serious bout of bleeding.

A few days later an official arrived at the house and told Nicholas he had come to take him back to Moscow for trial. The radical Bolshevik party had seized power in Russia five months before. Alexandra wept and prayed while she made the most agonizing decision of her life—to go with her husband or stay with her sick child. Finally, she decided to go with Nicholas, take Marie with them, and leave the other three girls to look after Alexei. At dawn the girls embraced their parents and Marie before they were taken away in horse-drawn farm carts. Then the three sisters slowly climbed the stairs to their room, sobbing quietly.

SEVERAL DAYS later, the train carrying Nicholas, Alexandra, and Marie back to Moscow was stopped in the Ural region. There, local Bolshevik officials decided to take charge of "the former

*The Tsar and his children sit in the sun on the roof of the greenhouse inside the guarded compound at Tobolsk.*

tyrant, Nicholas Romanov."

The Romanovs' new prison was a house in the town of Ekaterinburg. The windows had been whitewashed and a high stockade of wooden planks surrounded it. Their jailors ransacked their luggage and took many of their valuables. Alexandra wrote to the girls in Tobolsk and told them to "dispose of the medicines." "Medicines" was a code word for the Romanov jewelry. If they were ever able to escape, the jewels would give them money to live on. The girls then sewed hundreds of diamonds into their corsets and petticoats. In late May, they left Tobolsk with Alexei to join the rest of the family.

In the weeks following their arrival in Ekaterinburg, Tatiana, Marie, and Anastasia celebrated their birthdays. But there was little to celebrate with in the miserable dark house. Their food was often just black bread and tea or watery soup. Their jailors were rude and abusive. The family had no privacy, as the doors to the bedrooms and bathroom had been removed. Once a day they were allowed a walk in the garden.

After midnight on July 16, the family was awakened and told there was unrest in the town. They were told to go down to the lower part of the house for their safety. Nicholas carried Alexei downstairs, followed by the Tsarina, the four girls, the family's doctor, and three of their servants. In a cellar room, they were told to stand against the wall. Alexandra said, "There aren't even any chairs here." The commandant left and two chairs were brought in. Alexei was placed in one of them and Alexandra sat in the other while her daughters stood next to her.

The commandant returned, followed by eleven men holding revolvers. He pulled a small piece of paper from his pocket and read out an order ending with ". . . the Ural Executive Committee has decided to execute you." A disbelieving Nicholas said, "What? What?" The commandant pulled out his pistol and instantly shot him. The room then erupted in gunfire. Alexandra tried to make the sign of the cross but was shot before she could finish. Each of the guards had been told whom to shoot and to aim for the heart. But the jewels in the girls' corsets acted like shields, making the bullets seem to bounce off them and ricochet around the room. When the first round of firing stopped, Marie and Anastasia were crouched against the wall, crying and hugging each other. The firing began again until all the shrieks and moans had stopped.

*The remains of the last tsar and his family were laid to rest in this crypt in St. Petersburg's Cathedral of Peter and Paul.*

WHITE LIGHTS FROM television cameras lit up the inside of the church. On July 17, 1998, eighty years to the day after they were murdered, Russia's last tsar and his family were finally being laid to rest alongside their ancestors. In 1991, bones had been uncovered in the woods near Ekaterinburg. Scientific tests had determined that they were the skeletons of the imperial family and their servants. But the bones of the two youngest members of the family, Anastasia and Alexei, were missing.

Maybe they had survived! Until her death in 1984, one woman, Anna Anderson, had convinced many people that she actually was Anastasia. But when DNA tests were done, she was found to have been an impostor. This ended the hopes of so many that somehow, someone had survived that terrible night in the cellar in Ekaterinburg.

As the coffins were lowered, the rich voices of a Russian choir soared in a solemn hymn. Some of those kneeling in the church recalled the words of Olga, the oldest daughter, in one of her last letters from Siberia: "Remember that the evil which is now in the world will become yet more powerful," she wrote, "and that it is not evil which conquers evil, but only love."

# A PRINCESS OF INDIA
## Gayatri "Ayesha" Devi

"THAT ELEPHANT OF yours is just like you!" teased Ayesha's brothers. The elephant keepers, called *mahouts*, named their elephants after gods or goddesses and sometimes after members of the royal family. Unfortunately, the elephant called Ayesha moved very slowly and looked a little strange.

The keepers in the *pilkhanna*, the stables where the family's sixty trained elephants lived, also had a name for their skinny little visitor. They called Ayesha *pagly rajkumari*, "the mad princess." She loved listening to their stories and learning the commands they used when they rode their elephants. (*Oot* meant "get up." *Beht* meant "sit down.") Sometimes she persuaded a *mahout* to let her sit in his place on the neck of the elephant.

Although the *mahouts* enjoyed her visits, they couldn't understand the interest the Princess took in their lives. It seemed an odd way to pass the time for a girl who lived in a huge dome-topped palace with tennis courts (and twelve ball-boys to pick up the balls!), badminton courts, a skating rink, riding stables, and an enormous garden with a two-story playhouse and a swing big enough to hold four children.

Ayesha's father ruled the small northern state of Cooch Behar near the foothills of the Himalaya Mountains. It was one of the six hundred princely states that made up half of India before British colonial rule came to an end in 1947.

For many years, her family had been famous for its big-game hunts. Tigers, panthers, bears, and many other wild animals roamed through the state's jungles. The hunters—men, women, and children—stayed at shooting camps. Before the hunters arrived, servants put up massive tents with separate

*(Opposite) While many royal families own horses, Ayesha's family kept elephants, too. (Above) Her grandparents' palace.*

53

living rooms, bedrooms, and bathrooms, which they then furnished with beds, chairs, tables, and carpets. At night, a giant fire was lit in the middle of the circle of tents.

The hunting party rode on elephants to the camp. Because Cooch Behar was covered with swamps and with grasses that grew taller than a man's full height, elephants were the easiest way to get around. They were also used on the "shoot." In her memoirs, Ayesha remembered those special days:

"I used to lie down, my head between the elephant's ears, feeling the faint breeze as he flapped his ears, listening to the buzz of the bees . . . the sense of the jungle all around. I felt completely out of the palace's restricted life. Alone. Just me and the elephant in the jungle."

Ayesha went on her first hunt when she was five and shot her first panther at twelve. Today most of the Indian jungles have been cleared for farmland and the large animals are disappearing. But at that time many royal families around the world enjoyed big-game hunting.

On Cooch Behar's famous big-game hunts, the hunters rode through the tall grass on elephants.

PRINCESS AYESHA WAS born on May 23, 1919, a continent away from her homeland. Her older sister, Ila, and two brothers, Bhaiya and Indrajit, had been born in Cooch Behar, India. But Ayesha and Menaka, her younger sister, were born in England, during their wealthy family's long holiday in Europe after the First World War.

Like most royal children, they played with one another but longed to have ordinary friends. Ayesha remembers Indrajit unwinding one of their father's turbans out an upstairs window of their London house. It reached all the way to the busy street below. Indrajit hoped that one of the little boys walking by would climb up the silk "rope" and play with him.

Ayesha's memories of this time ended with her father's death in 1922. Shortly afterward, the family returned to its Indian palace. Her seven-year-old brother, Bhaiya, was crowned maharaja, and her mother—"Ma"—acted as regent. Ma continued Cooch Behar's famous shoots and became a renowned hostess, with guests—including Queen Victoria's grandson, the Prince of Wales—visiting from all around the world.

Sometimes, Ma took the five children to visit her parents, who lived in an even more magnificent palace. They traveled by train across India to the powerful Maharaja of Baroda's kingdom on the Arabian Sea. His elaborately decorated palace with its onion-shaped domes contained everything a child could want—a gym, horses, pet monkeys, their grandmother's delicious food, and, best of all, their grandfather's trained parrots. The brightly colored birds rode tiny silver bicycles and cars and walked on tightropes. They finished their show by firing a miniature cannon!

Beginning in the 1930s, the family moved

each summer to their house in Darjeeling to escape the heat in Cooch Behar. In this small resort town high in the foothills of the Himalayas, life was more relaxed than at the Cooch Behar court. But twelve-year-old Ayesha was always aware that she wasn't like the other children in her group of friends. While the others went to the movie theater by themselves, she could never go anywhere without a governess or a servant.

Of the three sisters, Ayesha was the most athletic. She liked climbing the hills around the town or walking the five miles (eight kilometers) to the Gymkhana Club, where the children roller-skated twice a week. When she wasn't walking, Ayesha rode her horse, her black hair tucked under a white pith helmet. At daybreak, she and her brothers and sisters often rode up a nearby hill to watch the sun rise over Mount Everest in the distance. Sometimes they hiked down Darjeeling's steep streets to the market, and Ayesha chatted with the villagers selling their crafts and vegetables. But her little sister Menaka always scolded her: "You can't do that sort of thing. Remember who you are. You can't gossip with . . . just anybody on the street."

*Ayesha shortly before she became the maharani of Jaipur.*

WHEN SHE WAS twelve, Ayesha fell in love with a handsome prince, who also happened to be India's leading polo player. Like Edward, England's good-looking Prince of Wales, the twenty-one-year-old maharaja of Jaipur captured the imagination of the general public. Jai, as he was called, stayed at Ayesha's family's house in Calcutta during the 1931 polo season. He arrived in a green Rolls-Royce followed by several grooms wearing bright orange turbans and more than fifty polo ponies.

Two years later Jai told Ayesha's mother that he wanted to marry her daughter when she was grown-up. "I never heard such sentimental rubbish!" replied Ma. But in 1940, when Ayesha was twenty-one, her mother gave permission for the couple to marry. On their wedding day, the soon-to-be maharani of Jaipur put on a beautiful silk sari, glittering jewels, and traditional bangles. Jai arrived at the Cooch Behar palace riding his bride's favorite animal—an elephant.

GAYATRI DEVI OF JAIPUR lived with her husband and their family in the Rambagh Palace in Jaipur. When India became independent from Britain in 1947, India's maharajas lost their power to rule but kept their titles and personal fortunes. Gayatri Devi was the first maharani to run for parliament. In 1962, she won an opposition seat in the Lok Sabha (Lower House of Parliament) by a record 175,000 votes. She won the seat again in 1967 and 1971.

After retiring from politics, Gayatri Devi published her autobiography, *A Princess Remembers*, in 1976 and founded a school for girls in Jaipur. She still lives on the grounds of the Rambagh Palace, which was converted into a hotel in the 1950s.

# THE LITTLE PRINCESSES

## *Elizabeth and Margaret*

"**I**DO HOPE SHE won't disgrace us all by falling asleep in the middle, Crawfie," eleven-year-old Elizabeth said to her governess, Marion Crawford. "After all, she is *very* young for a coronation, isn't she?"

Margaret Rose's tantrum about their costumes hadn't been a good sign. The girls' parents always dressed them alike. But on this special occasion Elizabeth's velvet cloak had a longer train. The cross six-year-old calmed down after being told she was too short to wear a long train. "Margaret always wants what I've got," said Elizabeth with a sigh.

It would be beastly if her often-naughty younger sister spoiled things. Papa and Mummy were already nervous about the ceremony. After all, they never expected to be the King and Queen of Great Britain, Ireland, and the Dominions. Just five months ago, they had thought they would be the Duke and Duchess of York forever. "Us four," as Papa called their family, had always lived a quiet life in their cozy London house. Then on December 10, 1936, Elizabeth and Margaret's favorite uncle had decided he couldn't be king anymore.

Less than a year had passed since Uncle David, the dashing former Prince of Wales, had become King Edward VIII. He hadn't even been crowned yet. During that time, he had decided to marry Wallis Simpson, a divorced American woman. Because his country and church would not accept a divorced woman as his wife or their queen, Uncle David announced that he would give up his throne for "the woman I love." He left England, married Wallis in France, and now lived in exile.

*Elizabeth and Margaret in their coronation robes (opposite).*

*(Above) The orb carried by the monarch during the coronation ceremony.*

It had been a terrible shock. No one had taught the frail-looking duke how to be a ruler. He burst into tears when he heard the bad news. The furious duchess never forgave her brother-in-law for forcing her shy "Bertie" to be king. Elizabeth, who was a serious, thoughtful girl, must have wondered what it all meant. She and her sister were royals, too. If they did something wrong when they grew up, would they be sent away to a foreign country, cut off from their family, and never spoken of again?

*After the coronation, the royal family waves to the crowds from the Buckingham Palace balcony.*

All such fears had vanished by Coronation Day—at least for the two sisters. Their father dreaded the ceremony. "I could eat no breakfast and had a sinking feeling inside," George VI wrote in his diary. Elizabeth also kept a diary, called "The Coronation, 12 May, 1937. To Mummy and Papa. In Memory of Their Coronation, From Lilibet By Herself." (Lilibet was the name she had given herself as a toddler and it had stuck.) Her diary's pages told a different story:

*At 5 o'clock in the morning I was woken up by the band of the Royal Marines striking up just outside my window. . . . Every now and then we were hopping in and out of bed looking at the bands and the soldiers.*

After breakfast, the two excited princesses put on their lace dresses (their first long ones), pearl necklaces, and purple cloaks. When Crawfie walked in, Elizabeth lifted up her skirt. "Do you like my slippers?" They were silver, although they looked a little odd with white ankle socks.

At the coronation in Westminster Abbey, Elizabeth and Margaret sat on either side of their "Grannie," Queen Mary. Lilibet thought she "looked too beautiful in a gold dress patterned with gold flowers." Queen Mary also wore seven strands of diamonds around her neck. After their mother walked down the aisle in her shimmering white gown with her maids of honor, their father entered the Abbey. Trumpets blew and the choir sang in Latin, "*Vivat! Vivat! Georgius Rex!*" The ancient ceremony had begun.

Aside from too many long prayers, Elizabeth found the coronation magical. "The arches and beams at the top [of Westminster Abbey] were covered with a sort of haze of wonder as Papa was crowned," she wrote. "When Mummy was crowned, all the peeresses put on their coronets. It looked wonderful to see arms and coronets hovering in the air and then the arms disappear as if by magic."

Back at the palace, the new queen complained that her crown had been very heavy. It left a deep red line on her forehead that afternoon. But the King had done well, and Elizabeth told Crawfie, "[Margaret] was wonderful . . . I only had to nudge her once or twice when she played with the prayer books too loudly." The family walked out onto the Buckingham Palace balcony and waved to the crowds below. Then they had to stand still for an hour as photographers took their official coronation portraits. A radio broadcast and a reception followed.

"We are not supposed to be human," moaned the tired queen.

IN THE MIDDLE of the night, one day in May, 1940, the alarm blared. Enemy airplanes were flying toward Windsor Castle. Servants hurried along the worn stone passages to the bomb shelter in one of the old dungeons deep underground.

But where were the Princesses? When they had first arrived two days earlier, the girls and their nannies, "Alah" and "Bobo," had been put in one tower and Crawfie in another. Alah was supposed to take the girls to the shelter. A frantic Crawfie ran back from the dungeon and up the winding staircase of the nursery tower. She could hear bombs exploding in the distance.

*Margaret and Elizabeth sit on the lawn outside Windsor Castle, where they stayed during the war.*

"Alah! . . . This is not a dress rehearsal. What are you doing?"

The very proper nanny was putting on her white starched cap. "We're dressing, Crawfie. We must dress," said the equally proper Elizabeth. Margaret was busy looking for a favorite pair of panties.

"Nonsense! You are not to dress," ordered the angry governess. "Put a coat over your night-clothes, at once."

Elizabeth and Margaret lived at Windsor Castle for five years until the Second World War ended. Many wealthy parents sent their children away to Canada or the United States to keep them safe. When asked whether her own children would be leaving England, the girls' mother, Queen Elizabeth, said, "The children could not go without me, and I could not possibly leave the King."

# EPILOGUE
## To Be a Princess

THESE STORIES OF twelve young royal women—from Mary Tudor to Elizabeth II—reveal that the "enchanted lives" of princesses happen only in fairy tales. Any one of these young women might have preferred to have been "a peasant with a baby at her breast," like the princess in Christina Rossetti's famous poem. Many lived in times when women were expected to defer to men, boys were valued more than girls, and parents arranged marriages for their children without their say. Yet, for the most part, these young women managed to overcome the very confining worlds into which they were born. A few, like Elizabeth I and Victoria, even became powerful monarchs who gave their names to the eras in which they lived.

Many princesses around the world today lead lives that their ancestors would have found unbelievable. Crown Princess Victoria of Sweden attended Yale University and has worked at the United Nations, while Princess Alia of Jordan, eldest daughter of the late King Hussein, is a world-renowned expert on Arabian horses. Others have won acclaim in sports. Princess Märtha Louise of Norway is an accomplished horsewoman, and the Infanta Christina of Spain was a member of her country's Olympic sailing team. Queen Elizabeth's daughter, Princess Anne, competed in equestrian events in the 1976 Montreal Olympics and is a member of the International Olympic Committee.

All of today's princesses work for charitable organizations, and some of them have championed particular causes, just as the late Princess Diana did. Although not of royal birth, Diana's elegant beauty and compassion for those in need made her the most famous modern princess. Millions mourned her tragic death. Her oldest son, Prince William, resembles her and represents the future of the monarchy in Great Britain. If and when he marries, his bride will likely become the most famous princess in the world.

Like princesses of the past, this young woman will have to learn what it truly means—to be a princess.

*Princess Alia of Jordan.*

*Princess Anne of Great Britain.*

*Princess Märtha Louise of Norway.*

# GLOSSARY

**archduke/archduchess:** a prince/princess of imperial Austria

**clergy:** people appointed to perform religious services

**constitution:** a document laying out a government or society's basic laws and rules

**corset:** a tight-fitting piece of underwear that is laced and hooked at the back

**courtier:** an attendant at a king or queen's court

**dauphin:** the oldest son of a king of France

**dauphine:** the wife of the dauphin

**dynasty:** a succession of rulers from the same family

**emperor:** the male ruler of an empire, or in the case of Emperor Francis, the husband of an empress

**empress:** the female ruler of an empire or the wife of an emperor

**galliard:** a lively dance popular in the sixteenth and seventeenth centuries

**governess:** a woman employed to teach and supervise children in a private home

**imperial:** a tsar or emperor's family was called "imperial" rather than "royal" because he was considered more important than a king

**lady-in-waiting:** an upper-class woman who serves a queen or princess

**litter:** a couch attached to long poles that is used to carry one person on servants' shoulders

**maharaja:** a prince of India

**maharani:** the wife of a maharaja or a princess of India

**mahout:** an elephant keeper and driver

**nanny:** a child's nurse

**pith helmet:** a hat made of pith or cork that looks like a helmet

**quadrille:** a dance for four couples popular in the eighteenth and nineteenth centuries

**regent:** a person chosen to rule for a king or queen who is too young or ill

**royal standard:** the flag of a member of a royal family

**scaffold:** a platform on which criminals are put to death

**soothsayer:** a fortune-teller

**tsar** (sometimes spelled **czar**): an emperor of Russia

**tsarevich** (sometimes spelled **czarevich**): the oldest son of a tsar

**tsarina** (sometimes spelled **czarina**): the wife of a tsar

**virginal, the:** a small harpsichord without legs popular in the sixteenth and seventeenth centuries

# SELECTED BIBLIOGRAPHY

Bokhanov, Alexander, Mandred Knodt, Vladimir Oustimenko, Zinaida Peregudova, and Lyubov Tyutunnik. *The Romanovs: Love, Power and Tragedy.* Italy: Keppi Productions, 1993.

Crawford, Marion. *The Little Princesses.* Toronto: George J. McLeod, 1950.

Devi, Gayatri. *A Princess Remembers.* New York: J.B. Lippincott, 1976.

Edwards, Anne. *Royal Sisters: Elizabeth and Margaret, 1926-1956.* London: Collins, 1990.

Erickson, Carolly. *Bloody Mary.* London: J.M. Dent & Sons, 1978.

———. *The First Elizabeth.* New York: St. Martin's Griffin, 1997.

———. *Her Little Majesty: The Life of Queen Victoria.* New York: Simon & Schuster, 1997.

———. *To the Scaffold: The Life of Marie Antoinette.* New York: William Morrow, 1991.

Kurth, Peter. *Tsar: The Lost World of Nicholas and Alexandra.* New York: Little, Brown, 1995.

Lever, Evelyne. *Marie Antoinette: The Last Queen of France.* New York: Farrar, Straus and Giroux, 2000.

Linnéa, Sharon. *Princess Ka'iulani.* Grand Rapids, MI: Eerdmans Books for Young Readers, 1999.

Longford, Elizabeth. *Victoria R.I.* London: Pan Books, 1983.

Luke, Mary M. *A Crown for Elizabeth.* New York: Coward-McCann, 1970.

Myers, Walter D. *At Her Majesty's Request: An African Princess in Victorian England.* New York: Scholastic, 1999.

Plowden, Alison. *The Young Victoria.* Briarcliff Manor, NY: Stein and Day, 1981.

Resh Thomas, Jane. *Behind the Mask: The Life of Queen Elizabeth I.* New York: Clarion Books, 1998.

Rossetti, Christina Georgina. *The Complete Poems of Christina Rossetti,* vol. 1. Baton Rouge, LA: Louisiana State University Press, 1979.

# PICTURE CREDITS

# INDEX

Paintings © 2001 Laurie McGaw
Text, design, and compilation © 2001 The Madison Press Limited
Printed in Singapore.
All rights reserved.
www.harperchildrens.com

**Library of Congress Cataloging-in-Publication Data**

Brewster, Hugh.
To be a princess: the fascinating lives of real princesses / by Hugh Brewster and Laurie Coulter; illustrated by Laurie McGaw.
    p. cm.
"Madison Press book."
ISBN 0-06-029480-9 — ISBN 0-06-000159-3 (lib. bdg.)
1. Princesses—Europe—Biography—Juvenile literature. 2. Princesses—Asia—Biography—Juvenile literature. 3. Princesses—Juvenile literature.
[1. Princesses. 2. Women—Biography.]
I. Coulter, Laurie. II. McGaw, Laurie, ill.  III. Title.
D107.5.B74 2001  2001024164  940'.09'9—dc21  [B]

10 9 8 7 6 5 4 3 2 1

## ACKNOWLEDGMENTS

Madison Press Books would like to extend special thanks to: Julian Dent, K. Corey Keeble, and Malcolm Ewing for their expert advice. Laurie McGaw would like to thank the following people who posed as models: Alexis Hancey (Elizabeth I), Gwynne Phillips (Victoria), Alyssa Roome (Gayatri Devi), Mallory and Marilyn Reeves (Mary Tudor and the nurse), Nicole Webster (Marie Antoinette; thanks to Emily Tratt for the dress), and also many thanks to Wendy Walker for her invaluable help with costumes.

*Book Design:* Andrew Smith, PageWave Graphics Inc.
*Editorial Director:* Hugh Brewster
*Editor:* Nan Froman
*Editorial Assistance:* Susan Aihoshi
*Picture Research:* Image Select International Ltd.
*Production Director:* Susan Barrable
*Production Manager:* Sandra L. Hall
*Color Separation:* Colour Technologies
*Printing and Binding:* TWP Singapore

TO BE A PRINCESS was produced by Madison Press Books which is under the direction of Albert E. Cummings

Produced by
Madison Press Books
1000 Yonge Street
Toronto, Ontario
Canada M4W 2K2

GAYLORD S